FROM A
MOTHER'S HEART

Toni Cowart

Unless otherwise stated all Scripture citation is from The Holy Bible, NKJV, NASB, and NIV.

Credits

Editors: Connie Geron, Betty Jo, Traci Ray

Front Cover – Brandy Wiggins (my oldest colored this just months before car crash)

Back Cover – Sara-Frances (Last drawing just a few weeks before car crash)

ISBN: 978-0-9912402-1-0

To book Toni Cowart for an event or share what this book has meant to you, please email Toni at the address below.

tonianncowart@gmail.com

Connect on social media @ cowartToni

Pursue Peace - Be Bold
Be Brave & Have Hope

Rom 15:13

Toni Cowart
10/25/18

~A STORY FROM A MOTHER'S HEART~

A STORY OF

TRAGEDY

AND HOPE

TONI COWART

Dedication

To my children, you have filled my life in a way I never dreamed possible. From the time I held my first baby doll as a little girl, I knew I wanted to be a mother "something fierce!" The moment I held my first born, I realized this thing called motherhood was far greater than I had imagined.

To my sweet friends, Mary Lou, Melissa, & Ella-Wayne, who in the early and raw days of my grief were "there" emotionally, spiritually, prayerfully, etc. for me while they, too, tried to wrap their heads around the tragedy that had just exploded in our lives.

To my dad who sat quietly by his "baby girl" and continued to be a rock for me during a time that he, too, was shattered into a million pieces inside.

Most of all to my incredible, loving and supportive husband Chris, who said "What's stopping you?" thank you for being a sounding board and encouraging me.

Thank you all!

CONTENTS

PREFACE

FROM A MOTHER'S HEART

It took the darkest time of my life for me to realize how precious hope is and to desperately want others to know that they are not alone and hope is real. I want others to know how and where to find the strength to endure what otherwise would be humanly impossible to endure. In sharing with you I am giving you more than just my story, I am giving you pieces of my heart. My story is not pretty. My history is peppered with everything from sexual abuse as a child and divorce, to living every parent's worst nightmare. My wish for you is that you will take away something that makes a difference in your life, a positive difference, one that can be life changing if you let it.

One crisp October afternoon many years ago a drunk driver suddenly crossed over the center lane of an Alabama highway while crossing a small bridge. The resulting fiery crash that occurred in those few seconds killed four people and severely injured another. Three of those that lost their life that day were three of my children. My life was forever changed.

How do you even...

Let me tell you if you will allow.

INTRO

She grabbed the phone knowing it was probably her daily call from her oldest daughter Brandy. Brandy had one child and called often to ask advice. She answered to find it was not her oldest daughter but Taylor, her oldest son. He was calling to say he heard she was having chicken and dumplings so he thought maybe he and the kids would drop by. She laughed and asked "Is this code for you are ready for your wife to get home from her conference or maybe you just love your mama's cooking?" He admitted playing the role of single parent while his wife was away to a 5-year-old little boy and twin 3-year-old girls was tough and he had a whole new appreciation for his amazing wife. That was ok. His Mama loved cooking for him, not to mention she would get lots of hugs from him and the grands.

She decided to go ahead and give the others a call and see if they wanted to swing by as well. Brandy said she would bring Jackson, her 8-year-old son, Sara-Frances the middle child, also agreed to come. Sara-Frances hasn't married nor has any children. Lord knows that child hasn't stopped long enough to hardly have a serious date much less get married. She was like that as a child, always busy, busy, and flitting from here to there. Her personality was a magnet and people flocked to her charming mile wide smile. She still doesn't "light" very often but loves to come see her mama.

Before the day was over 4 of the five children would be able to come home for an impromptu dinner/get together.

Gus joined them as well that evening. He and his little family live close by. Gus likes to share stories with his kids of their aunts and uncle; this always makes everyone laugh. Quite often his siblings turn the tables and tell "Gus stories" and this really brings on the belly laughs. The caboose of the bunch, Mary Alice was off in some country they all had trouble pronouncing. She was married to her work, or as Gus liked to say to dirt and a bunch of old bones.

It's dark, there's a bridge ahead, and is that a child?

Oh, oh my goodness, it's children alone in the dark. Wait, something's not right, what?   "Is that you?" "Taylor, you're alive – where's your sisters?"

"They're right behind me."

"I don't understand, it's been so many years, I'm confused, is it really you!?!"

"Yes, mama and we have been here the whole time, waiting on you."

"But I was told you were dead, that you all died together. I don't understand...."

"We didn't die, we have been right here."

"I don't understand..."

She walked toward them, heart racing, she was confused and excited! She could see her babies, all three of them. As she got close she reached out.

She woke with a start to another dream. She found herself wanting to go back to sleep and get to spend time with them again, maybe even get hugs and another part of her wanted to shake it off and not even remember the dream at all.

If only. If only reality didn't creep in and remind her it was only a dream. If only she didn't have dreams to wake up to - only to remember it was only a dream. If only she could really pick up the phone and call them, if only they could come through her front door to share dinner and stories of growing up.

If only, they had had a chance to grow up.

If only...

"If only" has been shattered by reality. "If only" could go even deeper -if she allowed it and sometimes she does.

If only she didn't have dark memories from childhood of her innocence being taken from her at such a tender young age.

If only she had been a good enough wife, he wouldn't shake her and yell at her; he wouldn't grab her by the back of the hair and pull her to the ground. He wouldn't sleep around; he wouldn't tell her everything that he found wrong with her. If only...

Reality comes with many faces and can be very abrasive. It seems to be the alter ego of "if only" and it can blind-side you. Sadly, I know this too well and there would not even be enough space here to write in all of mine. Raw reality has become my close companion. It has jack-slapped me into next week more than once and I do not like it one bit. It is part of the fallen world that I live in. I have learned that I can't control the painful rawness of some reality; however, I do have choices in how I respond when it reaches its ugly hand out to me directly.

Thank you for letting me share my story.

Chapter 1

THE BEGINNING

I didn't grow up in a Christian home nor was I taken to church regularly. I knew about God and I believed there was a God, but I didn't really know who Jesus was. I had heard of Jesus; had even seen pictures of the One they called Jesus. For that matter, I had also seen pictures of Elvis on velvet so that didn't tell me very much. I seemed to know more about Elvis than I did about Jesus.

To some this may seem normal, and to others this may seem sad. To me it was just ordinary because it was all that I knew. To me this was the way "normal" people lived. Without a doubt, I was one of the normal people. I did know some Christians growing up. I just didn't know that was what they were. I can remember if we were going to be around those folk, my mother would tell me I had to act "better around them" because they went to church, or they were "church" people. The Christians I knew were usually older people or women with small children. I do remember this one family though. Yeah, it was a whole family; how wild was that? I distinctly remember that when I went to their home it was an incredibly welcoming home. I felt something there that I did not feel or experience in any other home. I wouldn't know what that special something was for some time.

After I was grown, married and pregnant with my second child, I began to feel this need for "something." Other than wanting to go to church I wasn't really sure what I longed for or what this needy feeling was. I just knew I had this desire to go to church. Now this was a big thing for me because I was shy and wasn't sure if I would know anyone there. Also, if you didn't grow up in church, you don't know the lingo and customs, which are very different for someone who had never regularly attended church. I finally took that big scary step and visited a church in my community. From the moment I walked in I knew I was in the right place. I felt embraced and welcomed. I looked forward to the next week so I could go back. Within a couple of weeks I was invited to Sunday school. I was eager. There was such a personal touch and intimacy in Sunday school and I liked that. Over the next few months something began to happen.

For a few Sundays in a row I remember feeling something different. Every time the pastor gave the altar call, I would grab onto the pew in front of me and hold on so tight. It was as though if I let go, something terrible would happen. I felt like wild horses could not drag me down that aisle. Then one Sunday it was as if wild horses could not hold me in place. I don't even remember what the pastor said. I just remember I had to go. I knew that it was this One they call Jesus that I wanted to lead my life. I can't really explain how I knew I needed Him so much; I just did. Little did I know just how much my life had just changed! As I exited the church that day the pastor shook my hand and told me he had been praying for me and that he felt like the Holy Spirit had been working. I remember thinking- *what in the devil is the Holy Spirit*?!

Not being raised in the church, I had a lot of naivety where "church or Christian things" were concerned. I don't consider myself someone very savvy when it comes to street smarts, but it is amazing that once you belong to Jesus Christ; He gives you something even better--"heart smarts." For example: During the course of the next week as I would run into people from the church and they would tell me how glad they were that I had "joined the church" or were tickled that I had become a member of their church. Well, I was proud to be a member of their church and proud I had joined it, but let me tell you – that didn't have squat to do with why I went down the aisle that day! I may not have been able to articulate what had happened very eloquently; but in my heart, I knew it was special and different. That was the major turning point in my life.

Chapter 2

MY FAMILY

Fast forward many years, toils, and five children later. I thought I had the world by the tail. I loved my big family. You know, people are funny. If you have two kids they think that's great, if you have three, it's, "Wow, you have three kids!" If you have four they think you are crazy, and have you lost your mind? By the time you have five they just assume that you're crazy and don't even bother to comment anymore; they only stare. We loved our big family. The bigger the better!

There was my first-born, a daughter, Brandy-- blonde hair, and blue eyes, quiet, mild mannered and just plain sweet. Then there was my oldest son, Taylor-- second in line, blonde hair, big blue eyes, very mischievous, loved to pull pranks on people and then just roll with laughter, usually on their behalf. Next we had Sara-Frances. She was my pistol, always wide open, outgoing, never met a stranger, blue eyes and a smile a mile wide. Gus was my fourth child, blonde hair, blue eyes and he so loved his big brother and sissies, and was into everything! Mary Alice, the caboose-- blonde curls, blue eyes, and definitely her own little person. There is nothing more precious to a mother than her children.

I don't mean to leave fathers out of this. It's just that I am not a man so I can't tell you how they feel. I only know how I, as a female, a woman, and mother, feel.

Women are by nature very passionate creatures. And I

believe that when we become mothers that passion is magnified. I will never forget the birth of my first child. All of my children are special, but there is just something about that first one. She was so perfect to me, even the way she smelled. I remember just sitting and staring at her for long moments at a time and thinking how perfectly she was formed. I thought every little thing she did was so precious and beautiful and cute all rolled into one.

Fifteen months later I was pregnant with our second child, so when he was born they were two years and three days apart. Again, I marveled at how perfect he was. At this point I did know my Lord and Savior and I was amazed at how many different ways my baby son was unique.

A mere twenty-one months later my Sara-Frances came along.

There was a miscarriage between number three and four. The miscarriage hit me out of left field. We were so excited about this baby only to lose it. That was very difficult to deal with. I found it very hard for people to know how to deal with me. I had lost something so precious to me, and yet it was something they couldn't see or touch. The loss was real, the emotions that were evoked were real, and it really was difficult for me when people just wanted me to get back to "life."

Then here came Gus, so with the miscarriage we now had a four-year gap between babies. But only thirteen months later Mary Alice arrived.

I carried these children for nine months, gave birth to them, nursed them, held them, rocked them, laughed with them, spanked them, cried with them, and loved them more than the air I breathed. Don't get me wrong, with five kids life can get chaotic, busy, and downright crazy at times. But I loved every moment and believe me, there was never a dull second! Let me give you a couple of 'for instances'.

I kept telling myself they were such typical kids. I remember when Brandy was about three and Taylor one, she had made a little hole in the ground in the back yard, and she put some water in it and stirred it up, nice and muddy. Then she told Taylor it was chocolate milk. I caught him, just before his little lips got to his special drink his big sissy had made him. Thank goodness I was close enough to stop that!

One day we were leaving to go visit my parents which would be an all day trip. Before leaving Taylor had been catching roly polies and putting them in a bowl. As we left that day the bowl was set on the floor and forgotten on our way out. One of Sara-Frances' favorite foods was Kix cereal, which she had eaten some that morning. Once arriving back home that evening, tired and ready to unload and settle into home, the first person I carried in was Sara-Frances. She was about eight or nine months old. As I was unloading, I would talk to her and smile as I would walk back and forth. On one of my trips walking by, when she smiled I noticed she had black around her few teeth. I stopped, leaned down to check her mouth only to find she had been sitting there eating the bowl of roly polies from that morning. I guess she thought they were a different flavor of Kix cereal.

This was October 1995; Gus was still a newborn and the older kids were in love with him. They thought he was the greatest thing since legos and Barbie dolls and to them the best part was, he belonged to us.

I always loved to lay my babies on a pallet on the floor and the fourth baby was no exception. He was lying on his blanket in our great room which was in our sunken den, with the kitchen overlooking. This was perfect for me being in the kitchen and getting to monitor all that was going on in the den. I had stepped into the laundry room to tend to some clothes and upon my return, I found Brandy, Taylor and Sara-Frances all lining up and taking turns jumping over their new baby brother. They were excited over the new game they had come up with while I was horrified. I told them they could NOT do this. Sincerely they informed me they were being careful and he was having fun, too.

With kids, or should I say with a Gus in the house, things can go from calm to chaotic in mere seconds. This was November 2001. The night began with a peaceful setting, not for long though. It was a Wednesday evening and all seemed well throughout our home. One may have even used the word serene. My husband was reading the newspaper; Gus, six at the time, was working on a puzzle at the coffee table and Mary Alice his younger sister, age five, was working on her puzzle on the floor. Everyone was within reaching distance of one another. I myself could not help but make a mental note of how sweet the kids looked as I headed to take my shower.

As I stepped out of my shower I noticed that Gus had slipped a small rubber snake under the bathroom door. Knowing that my son would want some sort of rouse out of his mother, I headed to the den to pretend he'd scared the wits out of me.

On not seeing him right off, and assuming he was now playing in his sisters room (I saw her light on which was not on before), I decided not to disturb him just yet and instead go and blow dry my hair. On my way back to the bathroom I noticed the back door was unlocked. Considering it was already dark, I locked the door.

Once I had finished drying my hair, I returned to the den once again to let Gus know that his snake had really scared mama and watch him giggle and grin. On not seeing him, I headed to Mary Alice's room. No sight of Gus. I glanced around the place, no Gus.

I went back to the den and asked my husband, "where's Gus?" "Around here somewhere" came the reply. After calling for him and having another "look around" for him didn't turn anything up, we began to look in earnest.

My husband went to the back door and returned with the reply, "I know he didn't go outside because the door is locked."

Now, don't I feel bad! I have just possibly locked my child outside before drying my hair, my poor child! We headed outside and began to look and call for him. After no response, we returned back to the house and did a more thorough search of the house for him.

We checked under beds, in closets, in cabinets, any nook or cranny we thought was possible for him to be. I even remember opening the microwave and then shaking my head because I had even looked in such a place (but I also knew my Gus). So we looked, and we re- looked. The whole time we were yelling for him. Nothing.

My husband called some friends from down the road to help us look for him. They too searched inside and out. My husband then called the Sheriff's department, who in turn sent out deputies.

So many people showed up in our yard to help search, I'm not even sure I could tell you how many! They were in the house searching, in the yard, and in the woods. Dogs were being sent to help track him; so "our search party" was called off so we would not interfere with the scent. When we were told they would need a piece of clothing that Gus had worn recently, the reality really hit of how one minute all seemed fine and the next it was unreal. All I could think was, "all I did was get in the shower!"

People were arriving in a steady stream. All were ready to help. Some of whom we didn't even know. Our local channel NEWS FIVE had contacted the sheriff's department and offered the use of their Helicopter. The FBI had just phoned and my husband was speaking with them when another deputy arrived.

As I saw one of the deputies enter into my den he made a general sweep with his eyes as he chose a place to begin his search. He headed to our bedroom, bent down and immediately found him the first place he looked, under the corner of our bed!

I can name five people off the top of my head, including myself that looked under that bed. I know for a fact that some of those people looked more than once! It was a flood of relief and yet I'll admit very embarrassing that he was found so easy.

The deputy upon seeing my son's boots asked, "Is this the child that's lost?" I have to admit that even in my frantic moment the thought that went through my head was "naw, that must be the kid we misplaced last week, of course that's him!"

Now, did God place that sleeping child under that bed, or did the little turkey fall asleep while waiting to scare his mama with a rubber snake? My neighbor believes the first but only God himself may know the answer to that; but that's O.K. because we have our stinker of a son back.

We pulled him out. He was sound asleep and after hugging the "dickens" out of him, we put him to bed. The next morning when asked about the whole ordeal, all he could remember was placing the snake under my door, nothing else.

Never a dull moment!

Chapter 3

BACKTRACKING

I need to backtrack for a moment and fill in some blanks. This part of my story is both difficult and healing for me. Earlier, I left out some important things that should be shared. For one thing, it will help some of this make a little more sense. Secondly, there may be someone out there who is experiencing some similar situations and may just need to know they are not alone in the world. You see, in life we aren't always allotted one tragedy per person.

My first tragedy began at a very young age. I was somewhere around age six when my childhood turned confusing for me. A trusted family member began sexually abusing me. I remember the first time so vividly and for a long time carried enormous guilt. The shame was so heavy I convinced myself I would never be like other little girls. Most of the guilt came from the fact that it was me, my very own self, who had asked could I spend that night at his house. His wife was in the hospital and we had always spent so much time in their home. Well, I just didn't think anything about it. I remember begging to go. I can even remember my parents asking him if he was he sure it would be okay with his wife being away. Wouldn't I be in the way?

I was so excited that I was getting to go. Little did I know that what happened that night in the house would take place many times later in their woodshed. I once had a pastor who used to joke about misbehaving and being sent to the woodshed. That never brought a laugh to me because the woodshed was another fear for me. Somewhere around age ten to eleven it all just stopped, and soon after we moved many miles away from this family. It was probably another couple of years before I was brave enough to tell someone what had happened.

My next major turmoil in life came just a few months after I was married and was pregnant with my first child.

I call this major turmoil because we have so many upsetting times in life that at the moment they are happening, we think they are the very worst. We learn a little down the road that they were really just small bumps and curves along the journey.

I married my first husband fresh out of school; we had a beautiful wedding. It was like a dream come true. We tried to get pregnant for quite some time. Finally, we were going to have a baby. I didn't think I could be any happier. A few months into the pregnancy something went terribly wrong, not with the baby, but with our marriage. My husband became verbally abusive; this slowly mushroomed into mental abuse and then physical.

I didn't understand. I believed him every time he told me it was my fault. I thought if I could just do things right, or even just better, we would make it. Our second child was conceived with me believing he was so sorry about the first affair he had. He wanted us to have another baby and said I would see how things would be different. Over the next three years he had more affairs and developed a gambling problem. It seemed he was ruled by drugs and alcohol. It was a sad time. When our third child was born, he went into rehab. The first five months he was home everything was so wonderful again. Then back down the slippery slope he fell. He was once again engulfed in his previous way of life.

His own brother asked me how I could have had three children with him if things were so bad. This was a very good question. When you love someone so much and you truly want them to turn their life around, sometimes you just want so very much to believe in that person. I was in denial. I lived that way for a long time. Actually, it was my children who "woke me up" so to speak.

One day Taylor, not quite two, had just waked up from his nap, and I went to get him out of his toddler bed. I don't exactly remember what set my husband off, but I remember ending up between the toddler bed and the wall. As I sat up still stunned, I was eye level with Taylor who was so terrified at what he had just seen. At that very minute it was like this light went off in my head. Brandy was so used to this sort of behavior that she just stayed out of the way and was very quiet. So, what was I going to do? Wait until it was Sara-Frances who was stunned by what she saw and Brandy and Taylor both so used to this sort of behavior that they just stayed out of the way and stayed really quiet? NO! No more! I had thought for so long that as long as he did not lay a hand on them I could put up with whatever was done to me. Wrong! That is no way to live. I may have been raising my children to love the Lord but I was also raising them to believe this was acceptable behavior. Something had to change, and that change had to begin with me.

I am not advocating divorce. Please know that. I do know that God did not intend for us to live with certain behavior. If you are in a similar situation I advise you to seek Godly counsel and professional help for your particular situation. I chose to get myself and my children away and into a healthy lifestyle. We did get divorced and I do feel that it was best in my situation at the time.

Divorce can appear much like a death and cause a similar sort of grief. What helped the children and me was that we were already used to my husband being gone so much. We did not have to adjust to his suddenly not being there. We just didn't have to worry about what to expect any longer when he did come home. We didn't have to walk around on egg shells wondering how he might explode or what might set him off. We were actually able to take a deep breath and live. Don't get me wrong, there was still an adjustment period, but it was a good one, and we were happy and relaxed.

Chapter 4

A CONFESSION

I won't spend a lot of time on this, but felt I must assert some attention to this area. As a mom and nana to future generations I feel it is almost a duty to confess something here. I jumped from the frying pan into the fire.

You see, it is one thing to know God and believe in Him and another to truly trust Him in everything. It is not enough just to say you trust Him. It is one thing to raise my children to love the Lord and another to show them how to not only know His ways but to truly be willing to walk in His ways. Unfortunately, I have fallen short of my children seeing the latter in me too many times. That is something I am not proud of.

How can one who sees so much wrong in certain areas fall right back into a very similar situation? Thankfully I know the answer to that! You see, I knew what I was escaping in my first marriage and I knew for certain that I didn't want to be back in that sort of situation again. Yet I did just that.

Ladies and men, yes, men too! Men you are just as open to controlling and abusive situations as women. You must be so careful! Do you know the old saying "there is more than one way to skin a cat"? Well, there's more than one way to fall into the same hole! You may know it's there, but you still have to pay careful attention!

Satan knows us. He knows that for some of us, the very thing that is familiar to us is exactly what he can use to try to bring us down. He will use our old habits to work for his purpose, while going against us.

In the next chapter you will see that I married again. Getting married in itself isn't a problem. When you see red flags and ignore them, then you have a problem!

I thought I knew things others didn't. I thought things would work out. For the record, any time we, (me & you), think things are going to work out fine just because that's what we want to happen, doesn't mean it will.

Being in God's will isn't about what <u>we</u> want or what <u>we</u> think, no matter how badly <u>we</u> want it!

Being in God's will is about knowing that we are in His Word and truly following Him and aligning our lives with His will. By doing this we are willing to wait on what our God has in store for us. If we do this, we will NOT be disappointed!

The wait may be tough and even uncomfortable at times, but believe me, far less painful in the long run. Think about how great it would be not to be disappointed. Well, it can happen. And there is a confidence that goes along with knowing you are in God's will. I am not talking about a cocky attitude, but one that says you know that you know, no matter the outcome, your tomorrow is in His hands and all will be okay. It will be okay because of Him, not because of you or anything you tried to finagle. To know that God "has my back" and not just hoping he does.

That was a priceless revelation for little ol' me! Now, back to me falling for the same old same old.

Satan came to steal, kill and destroy. He has never strayed from that plan, (after all it works.) He knows what "gets us" and for many of us who are used to being abused, that can be familiarity.

Yep, that's right, quite often things that are familiar can very often feel so comfortable to us we are willing to slide right back in to a situation that may not be so good.

When something feels familiar, that only makes it comfortable, not right. Far too often we swap something good (because we aren't used to it) for something that is not good for us (because we are TOO used to it).

The old saying, "The fear of the unknown," is so true for me. Fear, self-doubt, and other things of that nature go right along with the same spirits of familiarity.

People, this is a very dangerous combination! As dangerous as that is, Jesus Christ is far more powerful. You can overcome through Jesus and have victory in areas you never knew you needed.

That is exactly what happened to me. When I divorced the second time – ughhhh, I still don't like that word; I decided it would be better to spend the rest of my life alone than to ever live the way I had been again. What I didn't see was that married or not, I didn't need to ever again open any doors that allowed things into my life that would put me into the same positions I had previously been in. I never have to live that way again, nor do you.

Chapter 5

A WEDDING

I re-met my second husband after I was divorced and we started dating again. I say re-met because we had a history together. We were childhood sweethearts. Our grandparents lived across the road from one another while we were growing up. We both would spend time at our grandparents' homes in the summers. We had not seen each other in many years when we began dating again.

We had a quaint wedding in an old country church that had sentimental meanings to the both of us. This is the same church the children are now buried behind. It was a beautiful wedding. Just a handful of close friends and family attended. Brandy now age six and Sara-Frances age two were both flower girls. The girls were so excited about the wedding. Taylor, age four, was ring bearer and was so handsome. Taylor did not want to be where he could not see me, so he walked down the aisle backwards, his eyes locked on mine the whole time. Sometime during the ceremony, Sara-Frances had nestled herself between us and just made herself quite comfortable.

To my husband the best part was becoming an instant father. He had never married nor had children up to this stage of his life. (Remember, I have slipped back into familiar and dangerous territory.)

At their tender ages of two, four, and six, the children began calling him daddy from the start. We never asked them to, but Brandy asked him if she could call him daddy. One day I walked back in the room and the two of them were both crying. When I asked what was wrong they both laughed and cried some more. They eventually got around to telling me that before the wedding Brandy had asked him, "Can you tell me one thing, can I call you daddy?" That's when the tears began to flow! The other two followed her in calling him daddy and that was that. He was Daddy.

He loved the children so much. He loved having a house full and immediately wanted more. Where ever he was and whatever he was doing he enjoyed the kid's right there with him. They were never in the way, just a joy. Believe it or not, this was an adjustment for me, a good one. It was still an adjustment none the less.

I discovered through this that love knows no boundaries, for it knows nothing of whose blood runs through your veins. Love does, however, know who calms you when you're scared, comforts you when you're sick and believes when you're told, "its O.K., Daddy's here." He may not have been their biological father, but he was their daddy in every sense of the word. With all of this said, it was very difficult for us when my ex-husband decided he wanted visitation with the kids. It was not in our original divorce papers. No weekends, no time in the summer, visitation with the kids at that time was not an issue to him.

In the beginning, they did spend time with their dad's mom who had been like a mother to me. The kids loved going to visit their mawmaw and pawpaw. After going back to court, however, their biological father, (my first husband) was granted visitation rights.

This was a hard time for all of us. Gus didn't understand why his "big bubba" and "big sissies," as he called them, got to go somewhere he couldn't. Every two weeks was a tough time in our house. Brandy refused to go for a while and then began to go back.

My ex-husband had remarried, and with that came a

stepson. I know the kids enjoyed playing with him while they were there. They liked their father's new wife, so this somewhat helped ease the separation for us, though I'll say minimally.

Chapter 6

GETTING READY FOR THE FUTURE

We were getting ready to build a new home. By leaps and bounds we were quickly outgrowing the one we were in and we needed more space. For instance, we needed a bigger table, a much bigger table. I used to hope when people came to eat with us that they wouldn't be too hungry. Somehow we would all squeeze around our little table and say grace. I am not sure how this got started-- it just sort of happened. No one wanted to be left out. Anyway, when we would say our blessing everyone would take a turn saying grace. Yes, even two- year-old Gus and almost one-year-old Mary Alice joined in. With Mary Alice it was more of folded hands mumbling and a quick nod of her curly head, and then we could all eat. It took quite a while for seven to say the blessing, especially as the kids wanted everything blessed, and I do mean everything from our food to our dog whose eight puppies had died. Don't you think for one minute that they didn't mention each puppy separately! So you could come join us for dinner, just don't come too hungry. (No one has starved to date).

We had been renting a cabin from some precious friends. We were staying there after we had sold our home and looked for some land where we wanted to build our new house. Our friends were very dear to us. It was while we were at the cabin that we discovered we were expecting the arrival of baby number five, Mary Alice.

Our friends were very excited about our new arrival to come.

The kids just loved having these friends as neighbors! Sara-Frances would often disappear, only to find she had gone to "visit" our friends. Taylor would pick cucumbers from the garden, roll them up in his shirt, hop on his bike and take off to share them with our neighbors. Brandy especially loved it when the neighbor's grandchildren came to visit. We had been renting from our friends for about a year and half when we found our land and began to build our new home.

The kids were all excited about the new house. Brandy wanted to pick out the color for her room. Once I had told her she could pick her own color she decided to tease me. Every so often she would say, "I think I'll paint my room _____." And she would always have some crazy color picked out. I would act shocked and smile while rolling my eyes like I had believed her. She would just laugh and tell me that really wasn't the color she had chosen yet. She would now have her very own room, no more sharing. The others would still share. They still enjoyed having someone in their room.

There was excitement all around especially because Brandy and Taylor had birthdays coming up. On October 18, Brandy would turn ten and on October 21, Taylor would be eight. They thought they would be grown. They were planning a huge spend the night party with a weenie roast and definitely some marshmallows. And party is what they did. That Friday at school it took my husband and I in separate vehicles to pick up all the kids and head out to our house. He picked up Taylor and all his buddies; I had Brandy, her girlfriends and of course, Sara-Frances, Gus and Mary Alice. After a night of fun with the whole group, the next morning my husband took the guys to shoot bow and arrows, ride four wheelers and just do guy stuff.

The girls stayed back home with me doing totally girl stuff like fashion shows, whispering sessions and having their nails done. It was sad to see it come to an end. (Mary Alice took her first steps this weekend.)   The next week at school they still talked about the fun they had all had. These were sweet memories.

That's the thing about memories; they are just that-- memories. They are of the past, not the present. Many start as thoughts or as dreams, then become reality in the present. Then they blend into the past, and that's when they become memories. For me, I feel like memories are one thing no one can take from me. They are mine and are so very deeply rooted in my heart that they are a part of my very being. Unfortunately, good memories don't protect us when life takes a turn for the worse.

No, life doesn't always go as planned. Sometimes that is good and things turn out better than we had planned. Sometimes they turn into a nightmare.

Chapter 7

THE PHONE CALL

One week later on a cool October afternoon in 1997, my life as I knew it came to a screeching halt. It turned into a nightmare, a parent's worst nightmare. After church on Sunday we had driven out to our new house site to cut some firewood. The three older kids-- Brandy, Taylor and Sara-Frances were going to meet us there. They had spent the night away from home at their father's house, and I had made arrangements for them to meet us on our lot for the new house. A friend of my husband's had come to help us. We had finished up and still no sign of the children. My husband thought maybe we had gotten our signals crossed and that maybe they were waiting on us at the house. (This is before everyone carried cell phones). We went back to our rented cabin to see if they were waiting there and maybe even wondering where we were.

When we arrived home, no children. While my husband unloaded the firewood, I began to give Gus and Mary Alice a bath. What I have not shared with you thus far is that I had an uneasy feeling all afternoon, one I couldn't explain. Actually, I had had it for a couple of weeks but it had grown much more intense that afternoon. We had now been home a total of fifteen minutes when the phone rang; I answered it—my husband was still outside. I asked who was calling and he said, "This is Buster Hough with the sheriff's department.   I need to speak to your husband." I ran to get him and told him that the deputy was on the phone and asked,

"If something were wrong with the kids wouldn't Buster tell me?" You see, we knew this deputy. My husband's face grew pale and he took off running to get to the phone.

I began to run back to the house, then, realized I did not want to get there so I slowed my pace to a walk... a death walk. There was such an intense feeling of not wanting to know what was going on and at the same time knowing I had to know. As I began to walk up the front stairs I could hear my husband literally wailing through the front door. I didn't want to go in, but I did. As I opened the door and walked through, I leaned back against the door as it closed. My husband was actually in another room, but I had a clear view of him from where I stood. As I stood there, I felt so overwhelmed by something, I can't explain it. My husband was sobbing so uncontrollably and then I heard him say, "My babies are gone, my babies are gone." At that moment I felt as though I couldn't move or breathe, and yet I could feel myself breathing.

My husband finally hung up the phone and came over to where I was and told me that our babies were gone. I told him he was lying and pushed him away. He was completely distraught, and all I could think was that there had to be another answer.

Deep down I knew the truth. I felt as though I was being sucked into the depths of something black, deep, dark and horrible and couldn't get out.

There are parts of the afternoon that I do not remember. (Shock has that effect on people.) I do remember at some point before "everyone" arrived, that my neighbor came into the cabin. I remember looking at her and crying so hard I could hardly speak. I remember saying, 'What am I going to do without my babies?!" She came over to me and put her arm around me. I had Mary Alice in the other arm. What I didn't know at the time was that she didn't yet know what had happened.

My husband, with Gus in arms, had gone to the neighbor's front door. When they answered it, he was so hysterical they couldn't understand what he was saying. Or neighbor thought it a good idea for his wife to come over and see me and see what was going on. I had never even realized that my husband had left the house. To me it seemed like the next thing I remembered was a house full of people.

The wreck had occurred around 3:00 pm on highway 84 in Whatley, Alabama. The pickup truck the kids were traveling in was headed west, back home to us. At the same time a car traveling east, being driven by a man on his way to his construction job, a man who was legally drunk. My ex-husband was driving the pickup truck which carried the kids. As he crossed a bridge, the car driven by the drunk driver crossed the center yellow line and crashed head-on killing my oldest three children. Brandy ten, Taylor eight, and Sara-Frances, six, gone forever. The drunk driver was also killed instantly. My ex-husband was seriously injured and was the only survivor. The vehicles burst into flames on impact with subsequent explosions following. We were unable to have open caskets due to this. Four people died in that horrific crash.

In the mere seconds that it took for the drunk driver to cross the center line, my world as I knew it came to a screeching halt. On Friday I had just picked them up from school and by Monday I'm picking out caskets to place them in. Something was so wrong with this picture! Even from childhood, and then as you grow up, marry and have children, you are subconsciously conditioned that you will most likely lose your spouse first, not a child. No one expects to outlive a child.

My world was now completely upside down. I wondered if I would ever sleep or eat again. I mean, why? All of a sudden things seemed so petty. As Monday morning rolled around, I knew we would be going to the funeral home to make arrangements. "Arrangements" what a tidy little word for such a life-altering moment in time.

I walked around in a stupor all morning. I felt like a walking zombie. Before we left the phone rang. It was the funeral home, and they did not need us to come just yet because there was a problem. You see, they did not have "that many" small caskets in stock and would need to get them in before we could come and look and see what we wanted. As difficult as that phone call was to take, I know it had to be quite hard for them to make.

So there in my den over the phone I had to choose caskets for my children. Who would have ever thought? Not me! It was just Friday that I picked them up from school and as we made our way home, laughing, talking, fussing, (the usual stuff on the way home) we had verbally picked out their cowboy outfits to wear to school Monday morning. This had been homecoming week at the high school, and each day at school they had "themes." Monday happened to be western day. So, here I go from picking out their little western wear to picking out caskets to lay them each in. There is just something so wrong with this picture!

It was a somber day when we finally did go to the funeral home to finish all the arrangements. We had several people there for support. Both of our parents were there along with my ex-husband's parents and brother. The wreck had occurred Sunday and the funeral would be Wednesday. My ex-husband was still unconscious and in intensive care. His brother asked if we could postpone the funeral a few days in hopes he would wake up. It was difficult knowing that he could not be there. At this point no one even knew what he remembered and how much they would have to tell him. His family was dealing with the fact we could be burying his children, and he may not even know they had died. These were tragic circumstances all their own. We were not able to hold off the funeral. Due to the fire and small explosions the funeral home was unable to properly prepare the bodies. My ex-husband's family understood. We prepared for a Wednesday funeral.

Chapter 8

THE FUNERAL

The day of the funeral was just as numbing as the previous days. I will never forget the first sight I saw as we pulled up to the funeral home and got out. My jaw dropped, my knees went weak, and yet I was propelled toward them. Three hearses. I reached out to touch one and half muttered "three". I cannot explain what went through me as I saw three, long black hearses in front of me. Seeing my reaction, my husband says, "How else did you think this would be done?" Well, to tell you the truth, I hadn't thought about it! To me it was another raw reality that three completely different, precious, individuals, three different faces, three different voices, had all been taken away. They had been taken away much too quickly with no time for good-byes. There would be no more hugs, no more kisses, no more "I love you Mama". I would never again feel the texture of their hair as it fell through my fingers while being brushed. I would no longer feel that sweet cheek against mine as I got that good squeeze hug before they got out of the car. No more.

The three caskets were at the head of the chapel, each one topped with flowers, and a few personal items that seemed to match their individual personalities. We also had a photo of each child atop the caskets. Brandy's had her baton trophy, her baton and some necklaces. Taylor's had his favorite cap, some deer antlers, and resting on the side was his trusty B.B. gun. I still to this day have not cleaned the speckles of mud off the gun because that was how it always looked. Sara-Frances' had lots of jewelry and her

30

baby doll. Not for the public, but for me I suppose, in their caskets I had placed a blanket that each one had used since they were babies along with something that had been special to each of them.

Their school choir, led by Mr. Michael Bedsole, sang, "Jesus Loves Me" and "Jesus Loves the Little Children". The Sullivan's sang, "At the feet of God."

The pastor from our church in Frisco City, Rev. Bro. T. Grant Parker, performed part of the service and this was very emotional for him. He had been with us through so much. Grant had even been at the hospital as Taylor and Sara-Frances entered this world; now he was there as they left this world. His wife and I had even had two of our children around the same time. We had shared a lot of things. This was one thing we would have been happy to leave off the "share list!" Our current pastor concluded the service for us. The chapel was so crowded, and many a tear flowed that day.

Even though I felt I was in my own little world, I also felt somewhat aware of the goings on around me. As we left to go to the graveside service I once again felt I was just rolling along in some other world. On the way to the gravesite something took my breath away the same way the three hearses had earlier. My husband told me to look. When I did, the first thing I noticed was the flags we passed were all at half-mast. The second thing was people coming to the side of the road, standing and taking their hats off to show respect. I didn't know many of those people and yet their hearts led them to an act that I will never forget and will be forever etched in my mind.

Even in my stupor, there was another site that caught my attention. In the midst of having passed so many people being still and reverent was a man being unusually busy. I knew this gentleman and what struck me was I knew why he busied himself and kept his back to the procession.

He, many years earlier had lost a son himself, a teenage son. As fresh as my pain was, I already had an enormous bond with other

31

parents who shared that indescribable grief. It broke my heart for him and a part of me wanted to stop and hug him and say "I'm so sorry but it really will be ok." Another part of me wanted to sink deeper into my own little stupor.

It seems so crazy that as overwhelmed as my whole being was, that memory is so vivid. I didn't realize at that moment, but I would forever share a bond with grieving people, especially those who have lost children. I honestly wish I didn't, but I do and I must say it's a special bond that only ones who have lost can relate to.

We reached the gravesite behind the small church we attended, the same one where three of the five children had been dedicated to the Lord.

Now three of those very five would be laid to rest. As I watched the pallbearers walk toward the hearses to carry the caskets, I remember thinking how hard this must be on them. They each had a connection to the children. Some had helped raise them through the church nursery when we were still in Frisco City; some, our children had played many a day together or spent nights back and forth. The main connection was they all loved them dearly. We had named, for the honorary pallbearers, each of their school classmates.

The sun was shining, but my heart was heavy, and so were the hearts of the Seales family. The Seales found the courage and strength to sing the song I had asked Melissa Seales if they would sing: "I'll fly away" by the graveside. I remember their beautiful voices; they were filled with much grace that day. They sang a cappella. Melissa shared with me later that after I had asked her to sing and she said yes that she really did not know how she could. She said she called a friend and asked how she could stand to sing when she was so broken herself. Her friend told her that if I could stand to hear her sing, then she could stand to sing, and sing she did. It was beautiful.

As the days went by I caught myself realizing that my life was upside down compared to what it used to be. I saw that I was constantly trying to turn it right side up again, to no avail. The more I tried to turn it right side up, the more frustrated I became.

I finally realized that my life never would be the same again, and that Jesus would be with me even if I was upside down. So I decided then and there, instead of trying to turn my life right side up, I would just learn to walk upside down. I would roll with the flow.

The struggle was over. I no longer had to try to fit into the mold everyone else thought I should. I never again had to go against how I felt to make someone else feel better about the situation. My grief wasn't about anyone else. Now, that doesn't mean that every day is perfect, but it does mean that I am equipped with the very power to see me through. Getting through it is far better than struggling against it. I'll explain more about this later.

I was sitting on the couch, my dad by my side. I remember saying to him, "This still doesn't seem real. I feel like it should be some other family and that we should be sitting here saying, 'bless their hearts'. What are they going to do?" But it wasn't another family. It was us, and it was far too real. I felt as though my purpose had just dramatically changed. Nothing would ever be the same.

Chapter 9

NOTHING THE SAME

To say my life changed drastically is an understatement! Half of my family was gone. I had lost more children in one afternoon than many people even have. For the record, I may refer to having lost my children; but I really don't like that term because that just makes it sound like they were misplaced like a set of car keys, and I know exactly where my children are.

So many people are affected when someone dies. In our case there were parents, grandparents, aunts, uncles, classmates, and the hardest for me to see every day were the effects it had on their siblings. Gus and Mary Alice had been affected in ways that would follow them the rest of their lives. Gus was the more troubled of the two. Mary Alice really didn't remember them a whole lot, as the wreck had occurred just one week before her first birthday. For Gus it was earth shattering. He not only remembered them well but had done absolutely everything with them. Gus ate, bathed, played and slept with them. He had his own bed but would end up crawling up in Taylor's bed. I think for him it was almost like losing a set of parents.

When our household would wake up in the morning to begin the shuffle of getting five kids dressed and three off to school, this was no easy task. The funny thing is we never really thought about it. Things just seemed to flow. Yes, we had an occasional "hang-up" where maybe everyone had to stop their routine and hunt a shoe, no small task considering how many shoes we had in our house. No one was ever uptight though. Everyone just seemed to roll with the flow, but now our "flow" was gone. It was never difficult to go through our "before the wreck" routine, and now just tending to two seemed so hard. It was not the norm for me, or for Gus and Mary Alice.

They didn't even seem to know how to play together. My husband and I figured this out quickly and were amazed because we had never realized this. When the other kids where here, they were constantly playing with one of them. Now they were gone, and it was just Gus and Mary Alice. They would look at each other like "who are you"? The older kids just thought their whole day evolved around getting home to play with Gus or Mary Alice. Now our house seemed so quiet. Too quiet!

Gus kept trying to figure out ways we could "get them back". We had explained they died and were not coming back but that we would get to see them one day in heaven. He just didn't seem to be buying into the fact they were gone. When we would pass their school where we usually got in line to pick them up, he would start calling them by name. He had done that every day when we would pick them up. I think he thought that was why they had always gotten in the car when they did because he had called them. So now I had to drive in a different direction because it broke my heart to hear him calling for them, knowing they wouldn't be getting in the van.

He would come to me all lit up with something he had just thought of to bring them home. For instance, one day he came running inside grinning ear to ear. Gus had a plan and was so happy. He very excitedly said, "Mama, we can get an airplane and just fly right up to heaven and bring them home." And the eager nod of his head told me he was ready to leave right then to go get them. It was hard to explain it didn't work that way; if it did, we would have already made those flight arrangements. He would spend hours outside looking up to the sky and talking to them. He would catch them up on what all was going on and things he thought they would be interested in. It was bittersweet.

One December he came running in the house all out of breath with another big grin telling me he knew exactly what he was going to do. When he could finally breathe enough, he told me that he didn't want anything he had asked for from Santa. Instead, all he wanted was his bubba and big sissies. He would just ask for them, problem solved. It was always so hard to explain once again that it didn't work that way. To watch him deflate just made me want to take all his pain away so badly, but I couldn't.

He had some very rough days. Sometimes I didn't know which was the hardest and most painful, seeing what Gus was going through or seeing Mary Alice not even remembering enough to know exactly what she had lost. She would never remember how two of them would reach in the baby bed to get her. They would end up tugging on her, both hoping they would be the one to end up getting to love on and play with her. I would tell them she was not a wishbone and to please take turns. The winner would triumph with both a grin and Mary Alice. The other would take a deep breath and see who was still available to play with.

Every year as the anniversary of the wreck rolls around people are so sweet to check on me and send cards. This means so very much. However, I have to tell you it's not just once a year that I am "reminded." That may be the time that many others are reminded, but for me it is a daily event. Not a day goes by without some sort of reminder. Every time I do laundry, familiar clothes are missing. At night when we all say good-night to each other, there are three less hugs, and three less "I love you's" to go around. As events and special occasions like graduations are planned, it is another reminder of who isn't here to do what. People have been so kind.

Each year our church honors our graduates. They have always remembered my three when it would be their year to graduate. That has meant so much for me. I have to say it is hard, but would be harder if they didn't remember. As the graduates make their way down the aisle, my heart beats faster and faster, and I always end up fighting back tears. The year my Brandy would have graduated, they presented me with a book they gave to the graduates. When it would have been Sara-Frances' turn to walk the aisle, one of her classmates presented me with flowers. This same classmate of Sara-Frances, Logan Breedlove, was so sweet. Right after the wreck the teacher asked what the class wanted to do in memory of their classmate. Logan raised his hand and suggested they plant a tree. He said that Sara-Frances was not there to watch grow up but they could watch the tree grow, therefore remembering her. I thought that was pretty profound for a first grader. The tree is in front of Gilmore Elementary School and occasionally as I pass

I will see that someone has placed a bow around the tree. That means so much to me that others remember her on special occasions.

Many times these events are sweet and bring a smile to my face, and others are like a slap in the face of what has been forever taken away. There are also some days when I can't even fathom what it would be like with everyone still here. For instance, the first couple of years after the wreck, I could still imagine what they would want on their birthdays. After a certain length of time, well, I didn't know what their likes and dislikes and desires would be because of their age changes by then. That was difficult to realize.

As Gus and Mary Alice reach certain milestones it has become sweet remembering one of the others reaching that, too. Then there have been times that Brandy, Taylor, or Sara-Frances didn't make it to that milestone, and that hurts. I look at Gus and Mary Alice who now are twenty-two and twenty-one. I realize I have no idea what my other children would have been like at these ages. When I took Gus to get his braces put on I was enveloped in the fact that Brandy's orthodontist appointment had to be cancelled because she died before the appointment date.

One day I was in Wal-Mart and noticed that a girl looked so familiar. When I went to get in my car the same girl and her mom came out and got in their car. Seeing the mom made me recognize the girl as one of Brandy's classmates. The girl got in the driver's side and the mom in the passenger's side. My knees went weak, she was driving, and my baby was not here to be doing that and would never be. They pulled off, in their own little world, and there I was trying to breathe normally so I could pull off. This was just another day in my life without all of my children growing up getting to do all the normal things kids get to do.

I have found that their birthdays are more difficult for me than the anniversary of the wreck. I am not sure why; maybe it's a mom thing? With each uniquely different child came a memory of a very unique birth and stay in the hospital. Each of those memories I cherish quite deeply. I can remember being in the hospital bed and not wanting to forget that special, time and I haven't. No matter how many children I had, each birth was just as special as that child.

I have noticed that this "mood" that I get in usually begins ahead of time, maybe a few days, and lasts until the day of their birthdays. It was strange for many years that instead of planning parties and picking out presents, I was picking out flowers to take to the cemetery. Once they would have been too old for theme parties it was a little different but not much. Somewhere around the second year after the wreck we were at the cemetery. It was a birthday, so we were taking flowers and just spending a little time there. As we got ready to go Gus stopped me and said we could not go yet. When I asked him why he just said we couldn't go until we sang happy birthday. Needless to say, it was a couple of minutes before I could even speak much less sing. As difficult as it was to sing happy birthday to them, I knew I would not rest easy if I left knowing Gus had felt a need to do this. I am glad we sang. It was sweet.

I will never forget the first time after the wreck that I was in a store a few weeks before Valentine's Day. Gus and Mary Alice were in a buggy. As I came up an aisle that had valentine cards and gifts everywhere, I became so overwhelmed. It seemed to hit me out of left field; I wasn't expecting this. I hadn't even thought of valentines and I round the corner and am surrounded. My breathing quickened, and my knees went weak. I had to grab the kids, leaving my buggy and just exit the store. As I got in the car and went to pieces, I realized how special that holiday was to school-age kids and could remember very well the many times my older ones filled out their valentines for their classmates many times. It was always such a special time for them, and they weren't here. There is something about every year, but that first year is the toughest! I believe that first year is roughest because all year you are hit with the fact that everything you face is "the first" without them. If the person who died was young, then you will be faced with what would have been "firsts" for them for some time.

Chapter 10

CHRISTMAS

A lot of people worry about me at Christmas. Now remember that for me their birthdays are harder than the wreck anniversary or any other holiday, but that first Christmas after the wreck was one that I wasn't sure would even happen for us. The wreck happened the last week of October, right before the holiday season. This doesn't exactly put you in a holiday mood. Thanksgiving had been tough and I was not looking forward to Christmas!

I thought Gus and Mary Alice were young enough, provided no one mentioned anything, that they would not even notice that we had skipped Christmas. Given the mood of the whole extended family, I didn't feel anyone would argue with me over us not celebrating that year. So I continued my daily routine with no mention of the upcoming season.

I don't know about you but when I am driving it gives me a lot of "think" time. Sometimes that can be good and sometimes it turns into a crying session. Either way my mind is at full speed. On that particular day something brought to mind a conversation that Taylor and I had a few weeks before they died. Taylor had been sitting up front; this was before airbags were in all vehicles. They would take weekly turns sitting up front in the van on the way to school. (You do know the front seat is the highly coveted seat among children!) It was his turn to sit up front and this always made great talk time for me and whoever was getting the front that week. The kids were all excited because both Taylor and Brandy had a birthday coming up. Their birthdays were just three days apart.

So preparations were being made and excitement was running quite high. Somewhere in the conversation everyone else's birth dates had come up and they had gone from excited to fussy at some point.

Well, as mom, I said, "That's enough; there are no more family birthdays until next year, so end of conversation." Things never end so easily do they? Taylor and I were going back and forth, with him saying, "Yes it is," and me with, "No, it's not." I decided to pull the ole "so prove it" routine. I asked, "Then just whose birthday is next?" With a very triumphant grin and a sparkle in his eye, Taylor declares, "Jesus has a birthday next!" My "I'm so right" attitude may have just been popped, but I couldn't help but smile too. I told him he was absolutely right. I think that child grinned all the way home.

If your child is going to "set you straight," what a way to do it! Remembering that conversation with Taylor did something to me. Jesus was born and Jesus died for us. If it weren't for Him, I wouldn't know where my children are today. How could I not celebrate the very birth of Jesus! I could not get home fast enough. I put up every decoration we had. I hung every stocking. Yes, every stocking. I still, to this day, hang all our stockings. My children are still a part of my life, and that includes Christmas. They just aren't physically here to help decorate.

The amazing thing is up until that point in my life I had always loved Christmas but there was always a letdown sometime that day. From that first Christmas after remembering the "conversation" I have never been let down once. Even later in the day and come Christmas night, I am still filled with the same joy and wonder I had when my feet hit the floor that morning. Easter has just as glorious effect on me too. Yes, I still miss my children terribly this time of year, just as I do all year. There is just something so different now, and it is something that no one can take away. It's what true life and death are all about, and what true celebrations are all about. I actually have children that celebrate the Savior's birth right there with the Savior Himself, and one day I will be able to join them too. I will be able to hear how the first Christmas really happened-- all the amazing details. I will probably laugh at how different it was compared to our version.

I now look so forward to Christmas each year, just as I look forward to seeing and holding my children once again! For me the most incredible thing I can think of to come other than seeing Jesus face-to-face, is to see all of my children again. I do realize that seeing my children will pale in comparison to the true amazement I will be privy to at that point. For my earthly brain, I have to think on terms that I can truly fathom. I can't wait to be wowed by my Savior. I can't help but wonder if He doesn't get a kick out of thinking about how we will react when we get there?

Gus, Taylor, Brandy (holding Mary Alice) and Sara-Frances

This is one of the few photos I have of all five children.

January 1997

Sara-Frances, Brandy, and Taylor

Taking care of a stray cat July 1994

Brandy - Easter 1996

Time to hide some eggs

Sara-Frances with our Lab Rebel

Taylor - there would be too few birthdays!

Poem Taylor copied for me in May 1997

45

Cemetery in Gainenestown, Al

This photo speaks for itself.

Gus growing up and learning how to go on without his brother & sisters.

Mary Alice -" the caboose"Will never know what she has missed.

~ PONDERINGS~

Here are a couple of poems I wrote the first couple of years after the wreck. I will save the others for another time.

A MOTHER'S THOUGHTS

I Heard the wind rustle through the leaves in the trees~

Sara-Frances, this made me think of how you once ran

inside and told me "Mama, the trees are dancing!"

I saw how green everything turned after our last rain~

Taylor, that made me think of how you always said that

green was God's favorite color. When I asked why you

thought that -your reply was, "Why else would He have made

so much green?! "

I watched as two butterflies landed on my flowers~

Brandy, this made me think of your most popular

question, "Mama, where do butterflies go when it rains?"

(Written in 2000)

TWO YEARS TOO MANY

Has it really been two years?

Two years of not tucking you in at night

Not kissing boo-boo's better

Not planning birthday parties

And oh yes, two years of that strong ache

That ache to just want to hold you one more time

Yes, it has been all of the above

But it has also been other things

Things that nothing else can take away from me

Not even death

Things like my love for you

And my precious memories of you

Some people don't like to cry

They say the tears hurt too much

Well, for me each tear or each ache of my heart

Is a reminder of how much I love you

And just how precious our short time was together

Whether it's been two years or two-hundred years

Nothing will ever be dearer to this mama

Than her children

Death may have claimed you three too quickly

But in my heart you will live on

You will never be forgotten

And until that glorious day when I see you again...

I love and miss you

Mama

(Written 1999)

Chapter 11

GRIEF (GOOD OR BAD)?

Grief is such a misunderstood thing. Or maybe we just don't want to understand it because it hurts so much. I do know from my own experience it is a very powerful emotion. Grief and love, I believe, are the two most powerful emotions; and when you combine the two (grief over someone you love more than air itself) it can be so overwhelming that you feel as though your heart has burst into a million pieces and parts will be missing forever.

Grief affects us in so many ways. But, grief is a God-given emotion, and I don't believe He would have given it along with our tears unless it was to be used! Now, I know some of you are thinking, but it hurts so much. Yes, it does. Now compare your grief to the love you felt for the person that died, or divorced (grief comes from many forms). Pretty strong emotions aren't they? I read somewhere that grief is not your enemy, and that is so very true! If it is not your enemy, then there is no reason to fight against it.

When you find yourself enveloped in this thing called grief you need to recognize that it is as much a part of your future as it is your present. Don't let that scare you, just know that it will take on different forms as you "grow" along this journey you now have.

The neat thing is that as long as you are going forward you are not going backward, no matter how small those steps are. You see, we can't afford to get stuck in a rut. Because then we are not

51

going anywhere, and in the long run that is much more painful than moving on. You will never get over losing your loved one, but you can spend the rest of your life getting through it. And that's a major key, continue getting through, or you get stuck in that rut.

Men and women grieve differently. So, if you have lost a child, don't expect your spouse to react just like you do. You each will handle what you are going through in completely different ways. That is okay. You each are different and don't have the same personalities, so it only makes sense that you would respond in different ways. There are healthy and unhealthy ways to deal with circumstances, but in grief I can't say one of you is necessarily wrong and the other is right. The key for me was to overcome my circumstances-- not to let them overcome me. This just may be the hardest to do in the loss of a child, but it can be done.

Closure is a word you hear often when someone has died. You may hear that something will give someone the closure they need. Sometimes you hear that someone was not able to get the closure they needed. Closure usually refers to the end of something or the closing of it. I found myself using the word in my thoughts and also found I did not like the word. I much prefer "healing process." For me, if you're healing you're getting better and what more can you ask? I feel that other people like the word closure because it makes them feel better about their situation. Not everyone, but many will use it if they are uncomfortable with your tears. They will say, "I don't think they have the closure they need yet." If you are doing remarkably well, they feel so relieved that they don't feel a need to tip-toe around you. This makes them feel more "normal" when they are around you.

Many people are very uncomfortable around grieving people. They don't mean to be rude or hurtful. They genuinely don't know what to do and are so worried about doing the wrong thing they may avoid you altogether. Sometimes they hurt too when they are around a grieving person. Therefore, by avoiding you, they feel they are avoiding your pain. I experienced many people avoiding me. It broke my heart for them. I wanted to track them down and put my arms around them and tell them it really would be okay.

Having closed caskets was tough. I don't think it kept me from having "closure". It was tougher when they called the day of the wreck and asked for the name of the kid's dentist so they could get the dental records for identification purposes. Yes, I believe an open casket would have been better. But if we could always have what we view as better, then I don't know if anyone would die at all. I have had dreams that they are still alive, and I believe those are due to not viewing them after death. It is tough when I first wake up because the dreams are so real. On one hand, it is sweet because I feel as though I just spent time with them. On the other hand it is almost like going through the funeral again. This is just another of many rotten things about grief.

When I had miscarried between Sara-Frances and Gus, I grasped at straws trying to figure out how to cope. It is especially hard when there is no funeral as part of the healing process. I remember just wanting to "feel" better. "Feel better" covered a lot of territory. Actually, I wanted a quick fix. One day I even called my daddy. He and I are really close and growing up I always felt he made things better for me when I was sick. It would seem as if when he got home, checked on his baby girl, gave me a hug, and usually brought me a little present, I felt better. Little did I know, a twenty-four-hour bug just happened to be gone by the time he came home from work to give me a hug and a gift.

As a little girl, to me he was the magic in the feel better. So here I was, all grown up, miserable and wanting to feel better – so I called my daddy. I don't remember saying a whole lot; I think he just read between the lines. He stopped by on his way home from work and brought me a bag full of "goodies." He had brought ice-cream, cookies, etc. He had left nothing out. I was so glad to see him. I wasn't expecting it, but after he left, I was even more down. I realized it wasn't "all better." It didn't work this time. This time it would take more than twenty-four hours to feel differently. It takes time to work through my grief; there is no "quick fix".

The first few days after the wreck our home was filled with family and friends there to help in any way they could. This was good in so many ways. Yet, sometimes people need to be careful and think about what they are doing and what it really means. For instance, washing dishes is great. However, be careful about washing clothes! I came in from making arrangements at the funeral home to find that all of the children's clothes and sheets had been washed. Brandy's, Taylor's, and Sara-Frances' smells had just been washed away. I could not bury my face in their sheets or pillow and inhale their scent one last time. That was gone forever. This person was just trying to help and when greeted with a hysterical me asking, "What are you doing?" she very cautiously said that someone had asked them to do this while we were gone. I wanted to cry.

In the corner of our great room, each child had a desk where they would do their homework. Every day after school they would come in and throw their jackets and backpacks on the desks until they got settled in for homework. The wreck had occurred on Sunday afternoon, so on Friday, there had been no homework. That Friday their backpacks and "stuff" had been tossed on the desks. So when I found someone trying to straighten them up I had to politely ask them to let me do that later. I wanted to just soak up where they each had put their own things and maybe even remember back to that afternoon. I wanted to go through their backpacks and see what they had brought home that week. It was sweet when I did. Along with books and school things; they each had treasures in their backpacks. Brandy had some notes and drawings. Taylor had some trucks, cars, and a necklace with alligator teeth. Sara-Frances had almost no school things in her backpack, instead she had notes and drawings.

I found that for me the thing that helped me was reaching out and talking to other people who had experienced a loss --just to know that someone else had been there and that I was not alone in the things I was feeling and experiencing. Because it hurt so much, my husband didn't want to talk to anyone. For me, in our home I was surrounded by such sweet memories everywhere I turned. Everywhere my husband turned, he suffered because of those memories. I didn't get angry with God over what happened. On the other hand, my husband was extremely angry with God and let God know just how angry he was. There again, there is no right or wrong way. In John 16:33 Jesus tells us, "In Me you may have peace. In the world you have tribulation, but take courage; I have overcome the world." In other words- when life stinks, God is still good!

If you are angry, that's okay, tell God. He already knows, but He wants you to talk to Him about it! If you are not angry that's okay too. The main thing is that you are dealing with it and not trying to ignore it. As long as you are trying to deal with what you are experiencing, that is a healing thing, and you won't get stuck in that rut of going nowhere in your healing process.

There are a lot of other things that go along with grief. There were many times that I felt like I was losing my mind. I was so thankful to find out that was normal. My mind stayed so overwhelmed with thoughts of my three babies I couldn't seem to complete normal tasks some days. I would forget things so easily. I would find the same clothes had been in the washing machine too many days. Or what I struggled with the longest was trying to cook. I had been used to cooking for an army, it seemed, and all of a sudden, I couldn't cook for four people. The only way I could cook a meal anymore seemed to be if I completely cooked one thing, and then moved on to the next.

That was the only way I wouldn't burn something and even then, it was not a guarantee. I just could not concentrate on one thing the way I should. I was so frustrated by this. It really was a comfort to find out this is completely normal when you have experienced trauma. I would often joke that it was normal that I wasn't normal. Trying to joke about things helped quite a bit in my coping. It was laugh or cry, and heaven knows I had cried more than

I thought it was humanly possible. One minute I would be smiling at the sweetest memory and sometime later crying so hard and couldn't even tell you what had set me off. I would just remind myself – normal.

I remember my granddaddy telling me how upset he was. My grandmother had gone through their home and laid pictures of Brandy, Taylor, and Sara-Frances face down. She could not bear to look at them because for her it hurt too much. My granddaddy would come through and stand them back up. For him it hurt too much not to see them. They went through this merry-go-round for a long time. My mom was okay with her pictures of the kids that she was used to seeing in her own home. She would come to my house, and the first room you walked through had tons of photos on the walls. She would shut that door, a door we never closed to that room. She felt too surrounded and it hurt. It broke my heart to see her hurt when she came over yet I couldn't stand for that door to be shut, so, I finally took the door off the hinges and that was that. Just a reminder of how differently people deal with things.

Something as simple as going to the grocery store was such a hard thing to do for a while. One reason is people would stare trying to figure out for themselves how they thought I might be doing. Secondly, I would reach to get something off the shelf only to realize the only person who ate that was no longer here. Or maybe it was this one or that one's favorite and could not bring myself to get it. I would be so drained by the time I got home. It didn't last forever. I still see their favorite things on the shelves in stores and just smile, (most of the time).

Having Gus and Mary Alice to take care of was some distraction as was our building the new house. They gave me something to pour myself into. I knew no matter how down I felt that I would be all right and to know that getting upset was part of it. For example; maybe while dusting or doing some task around the house, I would catch myself looking at their pictures and smiling over sweet memories. Later I may look at the same picture or think of the same memory and instead of smiling; just breaking down over what was gone. Sometimes in a photo if I just look at the shot as a whole, I think how sweet. Other times if I look closely I miss the texture of their skin against my face, or the softness of their hair, or the way they smelled at certain times.

That is when the tears flow, and the sweetness turns into a dull ache so deep down it's hard to describe. What would not be normal would be for everything every minute to truly feel okay. I believe that knowing I would be okay through all of this came from a peace I felt. No matter how down I felt or how my insides ached from their absence, there was this amazing peace I felt. In the midst of such turmoil, that peace was priceless for me. There are so many things that I have experienced that are so difficult to explain. I heard one time that if you can't explain it, God is in it, and if you can explain it, God isn't in it. That made so much sense to me. He is the only one who could baffle humanity with such things.

Chapter 12

FUELED BY PASSION

Passionate is a word that I feel would describe how most mothers feel about their children. I know it is an accurate word for me with mine. There is just something about a mother's passion rising to the top when someone has "messed" with her babies. Let that passion be fueled by a deep desire to know the truth about what happened to her children, and you have just met a woman who feels she can't be stopped by mortal man until she knows the truth. Or will die trying. I can't help but think when I look at my "fighting passion" for my children, how miniscule this must be compared to how my Heavenly Father feels for His children!

Yes, my children were gone. Yes, there was nothing that could bring them back. Yes, I knew the basic facts about the wreck. I wanted more. I needed more! I knew I could not change anything about what had already happened, but felt I needed details about the last moments my children had on this earth. Maybe it was a coping method for me, but I have always been a stickler for details and this was no exception. I was on a mission. I set out to find out as many details as I could. Not just about what happened, but how and why it happened the way it did.

I made phone calls and visits to anyone I felt may could help me. I kept running into walls. This was very frustrating. I did not give up though. I continued. I found that most of the people I contacted genuinely did not know how to help me. This was sad because for many of them, it really was part of their position in their job. I even, much later, found that it was my constitutional right to know certain things. I also discovered that by law within 72 hours we should have been notified or given some of the information that it took me several months to uncover.

When I made inquiries into toxicology reports I was even sent the wrong reports to begin with. I had anxiously been waiting each day for my mail to run. The day arrived! I saw a big brown envelope in the box and knew this was it! The long-awaited report. I held it ever so carefully as I trekked back up the drive to the house. Part of me wanted to rip it open and see results and another part of me wanted to take my time. After all, it had taken months to get this.

To my surprise when I opened it, it was not what I was looking for. It was two of my children's autopsy reports. I was not prepared for that. I just stared for a while. I wondered why they had sent these instead of the one I had asked for and if they sent these, why did they not send the third child's? I now had a choice. Do I tuck these away, or do I read them? I began to read. I knew if I didn't I would always wonder about the unknown. So I ventured into territory I really had not asked for. There were moments I smiled, there were moments I cried, and there were moments I just shook my head at exactly what their little bodies had been through. These reports not only give graphic detail of injuries, it's like they tell the story of what happened inside the vehicle. No, it was not pretty, but it was part of the truth. Now I had to contact forensics and let them know I still needed what I had asked for the first time, and I would like the third child's report also. They obliged with the correct information this time.

I can't help but feel as though God knew I needed to see those reports. No, it would not be for everyone. I knew my husband would not want to see them. But for me they were more precious, however horrific, details of my children. The more I know, the better I seem to cope. This goes back to the way people grieve and handle situations so differently. That's okay because God created each of us so differently. The hard part is not to assume that someone else should be treated exactly the way you want to be; they need things done for them in a completely different way. Being sensitive to that is not always easy.

The toxicology report of the driver of the other vehicle revealed that he had been drinking and was driving illegally drunk. I also found out from his driving record that he had a revoked license. So he should not have been on the road, period. I was unable to discover why his license had originally been revoked due to his age. When they were revoked he was still a minor, and those records are sealed. At the time of the wreck he was 26 years old.

All of this led me to get involved with MADD (Mothers Against Drunk Driving). Our county did not have a local chapter, so through the State Office of MADD, we started one. Let me state that drinking is not the problem. Drinking and then getting behind a steering wheel is the problem. I wanted to spread public awareness. I wanted people to understand what their rights were as victims if they had suffered such tragedy. Also, I felt through some of the public awareness, maybe someone would be touched by what could really happen and not drive drunk. That would be the real victory. The sad thing is you don't always see the lives that are saved. People who have come to me and told me the difference it made for them or someone they knew, helps me to believe it has made a difference. If only one life is saved, it is worth it!

I had received the other driver's driving record and found that he had been ticketed seven times from February 1997-August 1997. The wreck which killed our three children occurred in October, just a couple of months after he was last ticketed. Each time he was pulled over, given a ticket and allowed to drive off with a revoked license. That did not sit very well with me. I felt that each officer who had written a ticket, then allowed him to drive away without a valid driver's license, had each signed my children's death warrant. I was angry. If we had laws to remove driver's licenses, then how could these people still be driving?

There were many things I did not understand. I look back and find it surprising to me that I did not question God about "why" my kids were killed, yet I constantly questioned our laws, and many other things in our legal system. These were some of the things that I wanted MADD to help me make sense of. I spoke in schools to help our children become aware of the consequences of drinking and driving and of riding with someone who had been drinking. I spoke to many churches and civic groups all throughout Alabama, Mississippi, Georgia and Tennessee. Many teens and adults feel they are invincible. It's as if they feel that "something like this" will never happen to them. Many learn the hard way that it can.

I worked with representatives and legislators both locally and in Montgomery to try to tighten and strengthen some of our laws. I learned so much during this time. I have a new appreciation for our fire fighters, law enforcement, EMT's, etc. They each face a variety of tragic circumstances on a regular basis and still have to go home and be husbands and fathers. We need to pray for these people any time they cross our minds or paths.

When Brandy, Taylor, and Sara-Frances were little and we still lived in Frisco City, Alabama, you quite often heard sirens going down the road. It became a habit when I heard this to stop what I was doing and pray for whoever was involved. One day I heard a siren and as I turned around to pray I noticed Brandy, about five years old, already was praying. At the time, I just thought how sweet. Little did I know that one day sirens would be blaring and screaming and it would be us who needed those prayers, and people did pray. To this day I still meet people who will come up to me and say, "You don't know me, but, when the wreck happened I prayed for you". I thank them and tell them to continue to pray for me! It means so much to know people are praying for you. Don't ever underestimate the power of prayer!

About a year and a half later I received a surprise. I got a phone call from Kathy Sellers, who had been Taylor's kindergarten teacher. Kathy had been a very busy lady. There was to be a bridge dedication ceremony where they were going to rename the bridge, where the accident happened, in memory of the children. It would be renamed the Wiggins Children Memorial Bridge. Kathy did not tell me, but I found out later that she had been the driving force behind this idea. This meant so much to me. They could now be remembered by people who otherwise may not give the accident a second thought. Who knows, it may even get them to think twice about how they are driving?!

I have many people who tell me that when they pass over the bridge, they pray for me. I pass over it occasionally myself with different emotions on different days. Mostly I smile to myself and feel like my soul has just had a chance to whisper "I love you" to my babies. I know they are not there, they are in a far richer place than you and I can imagine. But, sometimes special places just evoke certain feelings in us that others don't, and for me the bridge does that.

Chapter 13

A MONSTER IN MY MARRIAGE

When we married, I didn't know that there were things going on inside my second husband that I would never fully understand. He had experienced his own things from childhood that would leave everlasting marks on him, and on others. Those very things had been eating away at him for many years. After the wreck, these things were exacerbated greatly. The monster in my marriage was growing. Let me note here that since the divorce, he (my ex-husband) has sought help and is enjoying a productive life now. Since that time he has also been able to spend quality time bonding with his children.

Throughout our marriage things had slowly been mushrooming just like in my first marriage. I found myself excusing so much. I would excuse violent outbursts because he had never struck me. That is a poor excuse! Throughout time others began to see much of this treatment and would ask me how I dealt with it and why I stayed.

A person can believe with all their heart someone will change, but ultimately that is not what will change them. Only Jesus can do that and ONLY if that person is truly willing to let that change occur. Sometimes they themselves are so comfortable and familiar with their own behavior I think they subconsciously would rather stay the way they are, even when their mouth says they want to change.

This is where you must look at your children and be willing to face what you have allowed them to see and experience. Having to explain and excuse their father's behavior to them over and over is not enough. Feeling like you must be there to be a "buffer" between him and them is no way to live. Knowing that when you hear his truck pull up, you morph into someone else just to be able to survive emotionally while he is in the house.

I had to face a lot of things that I was guilty of by allowing our children and me to continually experience these things. One of many wake-up calls was when I would go to take a shower or something and one of my children would whisper, "don't leave me in here with him." Their own father and they didn't even want to be in the same room alone with him. This broke my heart, but it was much more heartbreaking to know that I had let this go on for far too long.

I had to look my children in the eyes and ask them to forgive me. They were both young teens when we divorced and the sad thing was, as hard as divorce is they were so relieved to know we would not be under the same roof with him anymore. They were able to take a deep breath for the first time in their lives. When we moved out they discovered a freedom that had been missing for a good part of their lives. We all did. We felt as though we had been let out of prison.

My God had literally walked me through the valley of the shadow of death; He would now see us through this. And He did! I had a friend that asked if I wasn't afraid of how I would take care of us. If I had thought too long or too hard I could be very afraid of many things! But remember, God has my back and I know this! It would take a whole other book to share all the amazing ways God provided during this time of our lives. Not to mention all the people who let Him use them for us. God is so good!

Chapter 14

PAIN DEFYING POWER

I believe there are people who spend their whole lives in church and truly miss Jesus. The funny thing is that once you do know and understand who Jesus is, it is still up to you to make a conscious decision whether or not to accept Jesus Christ into your life. Earlier I stated that I was already an adult, married and pregnant with our second child when I came to know Jesus. I also said what a major turning point that decision was in my life. Little did I know just how much, during the years to come, I would depend on the very strength of Jesus to see me through. I am such a weak person by nature. I have found that is perfectly okay though, because I have a Savior who can do anything. Growing up I had heard the phrase "peace that passeth all understanding." I didn't know that was scriptural. I just thought it was a nice saying. Then after being slapped in the face with my worst nightmare, that peace became real to me.

I remember much later in the day of the wreck, telling the Lord that this burden was His. The horrible mess was His, I knew it was too big for me and I was not even going to attempt this one. Nope, He would have to see me through it! And He has not let me down. You see, from the beginning I felt a peace, an incredible peace, one that I knew had to be supernatural. It is a supernatural peace that defies pain. I was experiencing firsthand the true meaning of a phrase I had heard growing up. Who would not want a peace like that? The thing is Jesus just doesn't go around sprinkling it over

65

people.

This peace I am referring to comes along with having accepted Jesus Christ as Lord and Savior over your life. I mean truly accepting Him, realizing that you are just a plain down-right sinner--no if, ands or buts. He is God's only Son and loved you so much He was not only willing to die for you, but He did. And most importantly, He rose from the dead and is alive and well today! Only He can provide that pain defying power, and who doesn't want that?! As a woman who loves so passionately, I say we need it, because I believe that the deeper you love, the deeper you hurt.

There are things on this earth that are humanly impossible to endure. When you serve a supernatural Almighty God, you are able to get through things no other human would be able to bear on his or her own. It took the darkest time in my life to realize that God is exactly who He says He is! One of the pros of growing up without Jesus is that once I found Him – I found Him! I dug so deep into His Word. I didn't know that many people only pick up their bibles on Sunday when they go to church. I picked up mine and dove in on a regular basis. God showed me through His word who He was. I did not get "who He was" from a pulpit or someone else. I received "who He is" straight from God Himself. It never occurred to me to doubt Him. I was so new at all of this Christianity "stuff" that I didn't know I could try to put God in a box or try to make Him into something he wasn't. Today I am thankful for that innocence at that time.

With Jesus it is amazing what is possible. If you have Him, there isn't anything that you can't get through. That doesn't mean you don't have pain or bad days. But it means all things are bearable.

There was something God showed me that for me was quite profound. Not growing up in church, I did not have any old Bible stories or things like that, to "come back to me" during this grieving time. So for those of you who are so familiar with stories like Jonah, Job, Daniel, David and Goliath, it may sound trite to say I looked in the book of Job and found something to console me. I have found though, that there is nothing trite about the very word of God!

Anyway, I saw where satan went to God for permission to do what he wanted to do to Job. BAM! It hit me. God didn't cause what happened (So many well many people would say, this was God's will) and that was not "sitting well" with me. That was so big for me. Do you realize how big that is? Well, I'm going to tell you. You see, God is in control but he has given us free will. This world is full of sin and along with that sin comes horrible consequences. It was nothing but pure prime evil that instigated what happened that very day that my children were killed!

The God of this universe is so grieved over such horrible circumstances because His desire is for us to live, not to die.

I praise Him that He has the power to see me through such tragedy. Not only could He, but He would. When I feel like something has just hit me out of left field like this, (because I didn't see it coming), I've learned that God is never blindsided by tragedies like this. He not only knows it's coming but is there and prepared to see me through. This is one of the reasons I want God to have ultimate control in my life.

You see, God knows if we'll just lean on Him, or in my case cling to Him like a mad woman, then we're up for the task. How big is that?! Don't you want to be up for the task? I do. I don't feel like I have a choice. "Cause, boy, have I had some doozies when it comes to bad things happening in my life.

The thing about belonging to Christ is that you may get rattled, but you cannot be truly shaken to the very core. Sometimes I feel like someone is saying I'm not good enough or like my forehead should be tattooed with fool, sucker or failure; but that's okay, because on the palm of the hand of my Mighty God, my name is written (Isaiah 49:16)! That TRUMPS any name this world can give me! It doesn't mean that I don't hurt, weep or ache to hear my children say mama with their sweet voices. What it means is that I

67

may get rattled, but I can't be shaken to the core! Are you going to listen to the voice of this world, or to the voice of Truth?

1 Peter 5:10 sums this up for me, it says, "After you have suffered for a little while, the God of all grace, who called you to His eternal glory in Christ, will Himself strengthen and establish you." For me this says it all. Not if I suffer, but when. Not *maybe* He'll strengthen me but *will* strengthen me. We are covered by so many promises from the Lord of all if we will just accept them. Romans 8:18 says that I "should consider the sufferings of this present time not worthy to be compared with the glory that is to be revealed to us."

Unfortunately, trials will always be a part of life, (James 1:2-3). So how will you cope? It is up to you. You can choose to overcome the trial or let it overcome you. I hope you will choose to be an overcomer. I chose to be an overcomer. Satan will constantly try to convince you to give up. He will learn your weakness and that is where he will come at you. Satan is always trying to conquer. The thing is, satan is <u>trying</u>, but Jesus has <u>already conquered</u>! Satan has also tried to convince me that my days are numbered, well, in a sense they are. However, I have eternal life so if he wants to get real technical my days aren't numbered, they are eternal. It is satan whose days are numbered, my Bible tells me so in Revelations 12:12.

The Christian life is sort of like a football game. The difference is we know who the winner is. The true Victor is Jesus Christ. Life is just the game, so how will you play? There are many people who will watch you play; how will they say you did? I'm not talking about making some mistakes; I'm talking about your overall performance. Will it do justice to what the Victor has done for you, or will it just be killing time until the game is over. The stronger the trial, the more precious the pearl (1 Peter 4:12-13).

Chapter 15

NOT JUST FAITH, FACTS

People still come up to me and commend me on my faith. Don't get me wrong, having faith is important. I had faith in the Easter bunny when I was five. Faith can be very powerful. We need to be so careful what we put our faith and trust in. There are numerous scriptures in the Bible referring to faith and having "sound faith." I just feel that too often people get a "warm fuzzy" feeling or even superstition mixed up with real faith. So just know that your faith is based on facts! Galatians 2:20 says, "I live by faith in the Son of God, who loved me and gave Himself up for me." Ephesians 2:8 says, "For by grace you have been saved through faith," 1 Thessalonians 5:8 says, "Put on the breastplate of faith," Titus 1:13 says, "So they may be sound in faith," Hebrews 12:2 says, "Jesus, the author and perfector of faith." There are many more scripture references to faith. I am not saying don't have faith, I'm saying if you're going to have faith-- know the facts! Make sure those facts are based on the very Word of God, not on your neighbor's words, your parents, your friends, or mine. Check out the Word of God for yourself. Know the facts.

If you already are a believer in Jesus, don't stop there. You see, satan believes in God and even quotes scripture. I want more. I want to be a true follower of my God. In Romans, and Ephesians we are told to be imitators of Him. We need to be willing to conform to His image. This doesn't mean we never fall short. It means we are in constant "strive" mode to be like Him. There's an old saying, "Shoot for the moon, if you miss, you'll still be among the stars."

For me it is not just about faith, it is not about religion, it is about a relationship that is based on facts! Sometimes the simple facts are the easiest. For instance, quite often life stinks, but God is always good, and that is a fact that I will "take to the bank" any day of the week. See below for some other very important facts you should be willing to take to the bank:

Fact 1. Jesus is God's Son.

Fact 2. Jesus was born of a virgin.

Fact 3. Jesus lived a sinless life.

Fact 4. Jesus died for my sins.

Fact 5. Jesus rose from the dead and is alive today.

Fact 6. Jesus is coming back.

Fact 7. Jesus offers forgiveness!

I guess by now you may think I'm a babbling idiot, or you see there is some relevance to what I'm saying. I do hope it is the latter. If it happens to be the first, well, let's just say I'll wear the shoe with pride, (it does fit quite often). If it is the second, then know through all of this babble what I am trying to say, and know that it is straight from my heart, that not if, but when bad things come your way, there really is hope. No matter how defeated you may feel please know there truly is hope! You are not alone! There are people out there who would love for you to know that they share your pain, loss, sadness, grief, and despair.

Chapter 16

HOPE

But we do not want you to be uninformed, brothers,

about those who are asleep, that you may not grieve

as others do who have no hope.

1Thesssalonians 4:13 ESV

Hope. Yes, there is hope! I was not expecting the definition that I got from the dictionary. The dictionary gives the definition for hope as a feeling that what is wanted will happen; desire accompanied by expectation. The thing is if someone we love has died what we want is for them to be back here with us, so I think we have to go a step further. We know they can't be back here with us so what would we desire or want past that? For me hope is that I'll have the ability to carry on, to go on in a healthy manner, to have a productive role in life, that I won't become a vegetable to grief and despair.

We have all hoped in something at some point and time. The problem is – what are we putting our hope in? I believe people waste too much time looking for hope in all the wrong places, people, booze, etc. When we put our hope in things of this world/earth we will most likely be let down and disappointed. We have all had that someone who let us down. We must be very careful in what we put our hope in. There is only one place true hope is found, that's where I found mine -- in Christ! So, you may need to ask yourself where you are looking. We must turn to the hope that does not disappoint!

Romans 5:5 tells us "And hope does not disappoint, because the love of God has been poured out within our hearts through the Holy Spirit who was given to us." Romans 15:13 tells us, "May the God of hope fill you with all joy and peace in believing, so that you will abound in hope by the power of the Holy Spirit."

See, God wants you to have hope. I believe for us to have hope, it will naturally go along with our faith, but we can't truly have that without having the facts. Romans 12:12 says "Rejoicing in hope, persevering in tribulation, devoted to prayer". We are back to the fact that tribulation, (bad things) will happen. How you choose to deal with it is the real question. The ball is in your court, so use it wisely. Remember, life is the real ball game, don't just sit by and let the clock run down, make some impressive plays.

I also have the hope and absolute assurance of seeing my children again. Knowing they are in heaven and belonging to Christ myself, I will see them again. What a joyous reunion that will be. In the meantime, my job here is to use anything that satan tries to "blind side" me with, for God's glory. I can't help but think that when I hit my knees or praise my Lord in the midst of turmoil that it is satan who is blind sided - or at least squirming and undone.

Having hope doesn't mean you won't have bad days. It means that in the midst of them you can still smile. Even when you hurt you will know that better days really are ahead. It means that whether it is storming outside, or in your life that you can still say, "Yes, I am so blessed!" There are times that it may feel like it will storm forever - Rest assured, it won't! The sun will shine again.

Nothing brings joy to satan more than knowing he has you in a quandary over a situation. He loves to steal our joy, and especially our hope. If we belong to Christ then satan knows he cannot have us. John 10:28 tells us that if we belong to Him, "I give eternal life to them, and they will never perish; and no one will ever snatch them out of My hand." However, satan can wreak havoc on our lives so we are not productive for the kingdom of God. This is a way he can affect a lot of people through us (satan loves using God's people). Let's not let him have this. If we are not living intentional lives for God, then we are living for satan. Who do you want to be living for? Be intentional! Be intentional for God! So do what Hebrews 6: 18b-19 says, "Grab a hold to the hope that is set before us. This hope we have as an anchor of the soul, a hope both sure and steadfast."

In Him you not only will have hope, you will have a hope that is an anchor for your soul!

Chapter 17

REMEMBER

Sometimes life stinks, but God is good all the time. You may not know what is around the corner; just know that God has "got your back." Believe God, Believe God, and Believe God! We don't have to like or understand the things that go on. Just remember who holds you in His hands, and if you are not sure who or what you have allowed to master your life, then begin now praying for God to show you, but be willing to accept what you may see.

If you think you need to be perfect or even "better" to have a conversation with God, then you are wrong. In our fleshly peon, unworthy selves, once we belong to Jesus, God has covered us with such righteousness, such blinding light (that is not of us) but of Him, that when the world sees us they see plain 'ol us and sometimes our filth. BUT, when satan looks at us he has to squint or be blinded by the Light we are cloaked in. I love the thought of that! I don't really know what the spiritual realm sees but just knowing that both heaven and satan know who we belong to means they see something different in us. Why else would satan attack us so? I like to think it's the radiance and righteousness of Jesus in us (after all He dwells in us) and I believe that would make satan squint/, wince and squirm all at once. That suits me just fine.

I have lived with and through the worst of the worst and yet today I can smile and not just say, but know that I am one happy woman. I am blessed with a wonderful husband who loves the Lord and loves me in a way I never even knew was possible.

I have been blessed with the most wonderful children a mother could know. (Some I can hug today and some I won't be able to again until I get to heaven.) That's the best part ~ I will be in heaven one day with my Savior Jesus Christ.

Wherever you are in your life, don't give up. There is always hope and Jesus is always ready to walk with you no matter what your tomorrows may hold. There really is light around the corner if you are willing to look.

Chapter 18

HERE'S THE DEAL

Here's the deal...

If you are not saved you have two choices here, (a) take a nap, or (b) you can think about if there is something more you are wanting in your life? If you are saved, pay close attention because most of this pertains to you and will become a little clearer as you read.

So, you have now heard a horrifically tragic story. Now my friend let me tell you what is far more tragic. If you are saved and you have now decided to settle for just that, and only that, then you are missing the bigger scope of why Jesus died on the cross.

Yes, he wants us to have eternal life in heaven. Don't let getting into heaven by the skin of your teeth be all you accept! Jesus wants us to have, not just life, but life more abundantly. Can you even grasp what that means? I feel like He is disappointed when we don't accept all he is offering. He has offered us freedom, and not just a temporary freedom. We can live a life of victory, not just a moment of victory. But we must be willing to accept it, and then live it (be not just hearers but doers).

There is a spiritual battle here that most people ignore. It is real. Satan knows he can't have a believer back, but unfortunately he doesn't stop there. He uses believers on a regular basis. The sad thing is we let him! As believers we fall prey, or victim, over and over again to so many of satan's lies. He constantly whispers lies to us. When we don't know the truth, (and I must say sometimes we know the truth but don't use it), we just let the lies keep building. You know what I am talking about.

"You are not good enough, you can't do that, or maybe he calls you names, or tells you no one will ever know if you do this." Don't keep falling for this. Bottom line, he keeps us in bondage. Yes, he can keep a Christian in bondage. We still have eternal life, but not the life Christ intended. Many times we don't even know we are in bondage to something because it is so familiar to us or we have just gotten downright comfortable with it.

We would never think that we would be comfortable in bondage, but sometimes we even begin to wear our chains like a badge of honor. Sad but true. We sometimes even come close to breaking free but then decide it's too much trouble. Or we do break free and are so excited, but then, we decide we are more comfortable where we were because we know that so much better than this freedom thing. Satan is the one that convinces us to go back into our snug little chains.

Dear ones, there is so much more in freedom. But be careful, if you do break free and don't continue on that path, once you are back in bondage it will be far worse than before. In Matthew 12:44-45, the Word tells us that when the evil spirit returns and finds the house swept and clean (empty) it not only returns, he brings more; he brings friends! When you do that first bit of housekeeping you need to replace it with the right thing. Time with your Jesus, in the Word, this is the best way to fill yourself. Saturate yourself with the Word of God.

As believers we are called to be set apart. Notice I didn't say we were set apart, I said we were called to be set apart. We may be called to do things and then never do them, (which is an issue with disobedience). What a shame! I know you have heard the saying "God doesn't call the equipped, He equips the called." This is true, but we would probably fall out on the floor if we could see things from God's perspective and see what He has laid before His people that they did not accept. Oh, the blessings we miss, all because we think ~ "I got this." We spend so much time trying to figure things out that God already has mapped out. He just needs us to be willing and trusting, to be completely sold out to Him.

So we have this amazing thing called freedom that most Christians don't even take advantage of. Don't let satan keep you in a dark vacuum. Stop playing Christian, roll your sleeves up and prepare to get real about being set apart.

That brings me to this - Don't just be different from everyone else, be different for a reason. If we belong to Him we should be "set apart". So what does that mean? It should be a supernatural difference, something that nothing else could render except a relationship with Him.

That means you have had a life altering experience with the ALMIGHTY! It doesn't mean that you were raised in church and have been a "good" person all your life and never skip a tithe. Yes, you should tithe and I commend your parents if you were raised in church. However, many people mistake "all their life" familiarity with church and the lingo and just downright knowing how a decent person is supposed to act with a true one-on-one relationship with their Savior!

Also, having had that life changing experience doesn't stop wherever you were when you were saved. Praise God you have eternal life, BUT, to live in this world and be "set apart" we must be willing to die daily to ourselves, not just once in a while. There is a difference between getting into heaven by the skin of your teeth and being totally (sold) out to Him and being downright radical in your passion for your Jesus.

Are you passionate for Jesus only when things get tough and you don't know what else to do but call on Him, or only thank Him at an occasional meal, and always at Thanksgiving? Or, are you passionate for Him because He is yours and you are His. Are you willing to praise Him in the storm and in the sunshine? Are you willing to prepare for rain even if you don't know how long it may be before the rain comes? Even if others may get impatient or think you are off your rocker?

Are you willing to stand on what you know is from Him even when others are telling you to stand on what should make sense? If you don't know it is from Him, then by all means you should listen to reason. Here is the thing, if you have a close personal relationship with your savior and are willing to listen, not just talk, you will know when it is from Him. And if you believe, you need to be willing to STAND. If not, you are not willing to die to yourself and what others think and stand on what you <u>know</u> as TRUTH.

Obedience ~ that is what He wants. Through Him we are privy to a supernatural strength that is beyond our comprehension. With our Jesus we can do things this world can't. We have something they don't. We can have a freedom they don't even know how to dream about. This world is in one big power struggle and the funny thing is that with Christ, we have an inside line to "a beyond this world" kind of power, a power that can move mountains.

Chapter 19

TODAY

In spite of the scars that history has etched upon my very being, I am in an amazing place and I am happier than I ever truly thought possible. I am learning to embrace each new season I come to and that personal experience is priceless. We don't ask for "our story" but it is ours none the less. At the end of the day I wouldn't trade mine with anyone else.

God has given me the sweetest gift - the gift of beauty from ashes. Being able to truly embrace and enjoy life in-spite of tragedy gives me an incredible freedom.

Learning to live free and walk in victory is a privilege I want others to experience.

Break Free, Live Free, Walk in Victory, and Praise God that He is in control!

Romans 5: 3-5

...we glory in tribulations, knowing that tribulation produces perseverance; and perseverance character; and character, hope. Now hope does not disappoint, because the love of God has been poured out in our hearts by the Holy Spirit who was given to us!

Thank you for allowing me to share pieces of my heart

Please let me know what this book has meant to you

toniaNNcowart@gmail.com

@cowartToni

Personal Reflection Time

Take a moment and write down anything you are struggling with.

Don't worry if you feel it is small, nothing you are struggling with is insignificant to our Heavenly Father.

Do you feel it is so overwhelming and don't see any way out, that you should not bother – wrong! The bigger the problem, pain or hurt- the bigger you get to see God work.

And of course you could always take this space to list praises!

Then have a conversation with Him!

_____
_____
_____
_____
_____
_____
_____
_____
_____
_____
_____
_____
_____
_____
_____
_____
_____

Made in the USA
Columbia, SC
07 September 2018